Lena Holfve

Finally free from Fatigue!

Formerly ill, several since
fifteen years says...

ı

Förlag: BoD – Books on Demand, Stockholm, Sverige
Tryck: BoD – Books on Demand, Norderstedt, Tyskland

ISBN: 978-91-8027-583-5

Lena Holfve previously published:

In English:

Exhausted & Sleepless e-book, 2020 Amazon
Exhausted & Sleepless, soft book, (2020) Amazon
Bottoms up, e-book, 2020 Amazon
Bottoms up, soft book, 2020 Amazon

Lena Holfve is a Swedish author who made her debut at one of
the largest book publishers, Rabén & Sjögren in 1984.

Lena has several multi translated websites:
www.utmattningsskolan.se
www.utmattad.net
www.sömnlös.com
www.mögelförgiftad.com
www.parasitfri.com
www.cypernboende.com
www.holfve.se
www.lenaholfve.se

Table of Contents

Preface

Martina wanted me to share her story:

The book of Fatigue saved my life. I began to have anxiety; I was exhausted all the time, sensitive to sound, found it hard to sleep, was becoming more forgetful, and had all sorts of other symptoms. They developed slowly, over the course of two years, and got increasingly worse even though I was on sick leave on grounds of "fatigue syndrome". I tried every suggestion: meditation, leisurely walks, rest, vacations, etc. but nothing helped. I would get sick with panic disorders that could last a whole day if I did "too much". It was a major setback to my life. I had malaise, soreness in my chest, and I thought I was dying of exertion. Towards the end, I had such brain fog that I felt constantly intoxicated and I was basically bedridden. The doctors suspected Myalgic encephalomyelitis, chronic fatigue syndrome.

Barely a year after I started utmattningsskolan.se, or UMS the Fatigue school, I was alive again and working full time. I got my life back! ♥ I never felt so healthy and full of energy before as I do now. I have a normal life, exercise, meet friends, plan fun activities with my son, etc ♥ I had to take made a break for various reasons so now it's been 2.5 years, but I will not be satisfied until the whole school is finished. The tests show zero on toxins and I don't feel Fatigue anymore 😄💅 Lena Holfve can't thank you enough! 💜 Please share my story.

Martina describes well what happens when one is exhausted, and how sick and scared you can be because you do not understand what is happening.

We have seen time and time again that hope allows people to leave the belief that their condition is incurable and psychological. This hope is important because it fights the fear, and we have seen too many times that the fear can drive people to take their own lives.

I thanked Martina for that report. Martina is one of many people who were unknowingly poisoned by mold inside her home. The root of my illness was aluminum and parasites.

I started UMS the Fatigue school in July 2016, but it had never been part of a larger plan. I had shared a text about my own experience with Fatigue on Facebook and, to my surprise, it was shared by thousands of people. This drove me to create a Facebook group that was open for any interested parties to join; the number of participants soon reached several hundred. I quickly realized why the post had been shared so much and why so many people had joined the group – it was because I had been cured of Fatigue, and they wanted to be educated on how they could do the same.

Driven by their interest, I wrote the first course. While the participants of the group studied it, I wrote the second. The cycle continued until I had a total of nine sections, and Utmattningsskolan.se was born.

Now, almost seven years later, scores of people suffering from Fatigue have taken the course and are fully recovered. Some volunteers also speak about their experiences in the book. In Sweden, the symptoms are unfortunately often interpreted as mental illness. Personally, I never experienced this as I recovered in Asia, where it is acknowledged as a physical condition.

Over the years, I have learnt that there is a lot of overlap for those affected by Fatigue. Most diagnosis of" fatigue syndrome" were caused by metal poisonings or mold.

The signs are obvious – your eyes seem dull, you can't bear any overstimulation, your memory suffers, and you find it difficult to read or count. These are all due to the inflammation of the brain.

The effect on one's memory is quite startling. I remember, oddly enough, a moment when I saw car keys in the hall of my house. My brain was confused:" Did I have a car? And if I did... where does it stand? What does it look like?"

The Methods in this book have been recreated by me, and modified slightly, but they are all approved by the doctors with whom we collaborate.

Many people have asked me over the past six years why we haven't advertised or actively tried to spread the word. I knew from the start that the methods had helped me recover and that the recovery was long-term. However, it was only after many years that we could study the effects over various people. Now that we have many older members who have been healthy for 2-5 years, after suffering from chronic fatigue for 4-17 years, we can confidently say that these methods work nearly universally, and their results sustain over many years.

The root of the method is quite simple; eliminate the brain fog so you can think, get your sleep in order in a non-toxic environment, get the energy back, and then start looking for the root cause, using symptom lists and labs abroad to whom we send biological samples.

The book includes several videos, which can be found in its own playlist on YouTube.

The book often has gaps because the target group often has brain fog.

Northern Cyprus in July 2022

Author Lena Holfve

Anna is fully recovered

Anna had a metal poisoning, just like me. She was one of the members who photographed themselves before and after detoxification and, as you can probably tell, she is recovered now.

Unfortunately, many people can relate to the" Anna" in the left image; exhausted, sick, swollen, tired, long-term sick, and with an indescribable brain fog.

It is not always visible on the outside, but you are incredibly ill.

What is it like now 5 years later?

It has been a lot of fun for me to contact old members, who have been healthy for a long time, and who are through the whole UMS method.

Anna's response when I asked in April 2022:

"I am fully recovered now, working full-time as an assistant nurse and in the autumn, I will start studying to become a specialist nurse at a university. This is thanks to UMS and for that I am eternally grateful. I practice spinning a couple of times a week. I have energy and my life is in balance right now. Sometimes I fall a little but have learned a lot from school and manage to make it back on track.

I am eternally grateful to you for everything, and I will never forget the amazing help I received from you and the School of Fatigue."

Soon recovered

Ann-Charlotte's text is an online comment, but she has also spoken out in the local press.

This photo (on the left) was taken one evening in April 2019, in the middle of the dental job, and I was tired after a long day, but feeling and looking much more "awake and alive" than a few years back.

 I have received three fatigue diagnoses in 2001, 2002 and 2010 but became ill long before that. So, I had been ill for more than 20 years and continued to be ill even though I have:

– taken a course in stress management

– regularly done relaxation exercises and calming meditation

– regularly walked and exercised (when I´ve had the energy for it)

– eaten SSRIs, three times

– undergone cognitive behavioral therapy, twice

– eaten the best supplements and natural remedies recommended for Fatigue.

Even though I was a "good patient" I never got better. For many years I could not read and understand fiction. I joined

Utmattningsskolan.se, the School of Fatigue, just over a year ago and, thanks to the Golden Milk, I have gotten rid of most of the "brain fog" as it is called and nowadays, I read scientific and medical articles in English and understand a lot. I am on my way to getting well, thanks entirely to Lena Holfve starting UMS.

The photo was taken on the afternoon of May 2015, that was before I found my way to the School of Fatigue, and here it is clear how tired I was, because I don't really manage to smile even though it was portrait photo time."

How is it now, Ann-Charlotte?

I contacted Ann-Charlotte in April 2022. She had joined UMS the Fatigue school in 2017, so I asked her what her root cause was.

"I had multiple root causes and the first one I found was parasites. I followed the UMS Parasite Course in December 2018 and afterwards my 43-45 years of troubles with IBS was over! Medicine poisoning was another late root cause, and it was nice getting rid of the medication in the summer of 2018.

Then I think sunscreen and lotions was a small root cause, and nowadays I only use human friendly products on my skin, as well as in food and for cleaning and washing. I used to have a terrible itch from deodorants, and it took me half a year to find a deodorant without aluminum that did its job, but now I´ve found one that´s working and the itching is gone! I also had problems with my mucous membranes everywhere but most of my problems disappeared when I switched to just gentle natural oil and water, so soap was probably a small root cause as well.

But my biggest root causes were probably a root canal filling I got 2001, on top of a mild mercury poisoning. I remembered I suspected the root canal filling directly since I was diagnosed with fatigue only months after. In late 2019, I started getting good help from several specialists, and after many months with paperwork and phone calls, it all resulted in much of the cost for the dental job being paid for by the government. So, last year, I got all the toxic tooth fillings removed, starting with the infected tooth with the root canal filling, and after that I don´t have to take an afternoon nap anymore!

All the mercury fillings were then carefully removed and I didn´t get worse afterwards, which is very good! I know it´ll take some time to detoxify the mercury that remains in my system and I´m following the suggestions of UMS to help with the process. I am still lacking some energy and suffering from brain fog, so I will continue to search for root causes to fix. I hope to be fully recovered in a year or two."

Ann-Charlotte told me that she got bouts of itching and I knew that that was the language of the liver. Anxiety, worry, panic attacks and itching are the liver's way of announcing that it is in trouble.

In July 2022, we are going into our seventh year of UMS. Everything I have learnt over these years suggests that those who take the program seriously and go through it with immense care to detail are the ones who heal the fastest.

Kristina has a new life

In the autumn of 2016, I found UMS. This was when Lena had just kicked off on Facebook. For me, UMS was something that immediately appealed to me in many ways. Healing the body naturally has always been something that I believed. Lena has created an incredibly good "step-by-step" program that is easy to follow and take part in even for those with brain fog and cognitive impairment.

Personally, medication never felt like a viable option for me, even though multiple doctors had offered me prescriptions after my diagnosis. Sometimes, I accepted that they wrote a prescription for sleep medication or mood-enhancing drugs, but it was never something I even thought about picking up and using. I only agreed to avoid any confrontation. But for me, it has never felt "right" to "nibble pills" as I believe that these, in the best case, only dampen symptoms but do not actually target the root cause. Besides, I wasn't depressed. I was extremely tired, and my body and brain weren't working, but I had the will to live and the desire to do things even though I was sometimes despondent about my situation. So, I couldn't see why I should have to eat "happiness pills." I also believe that the cause can be exacerbated in the long run by taking medication to hide the symptoms that come with Fatigue.

Most people who have lived with Fatigue for a long time have probably started looking for different solutions and alternatives that could be what help you get healthy and become your old self again. \You feel very lonely, helpless, left out, and hopeless when you have tried everything possible suggestion, but none have worked.

As an exhausted person, you are stuck in your Fatigue prison and often must struggle with both the health care system, the Social Insurance Agency, the Swedish Public Employment Service, your surroundings and, in the worst case, even your own relatives. It is a "condition" that cannot be seen, unlike a broken arm, so some people are less likely to believe that you are truly suffering. Even if you can be lucky and have an amazing family, like mine is, that supports you and tries to understand you, it's impossible to truly understand unless you've experienced Fatigue yourself.

When I was at my sickest, I couldn't read, I couldn't have long conversations without starting to slur and "lose the thread", I was so immensely tired that I had to rest right after I had breakfast. Cooking was a challenge as the various steps to be coordinated were so incomprehensible and took such a toll on my brain that I often burned the food or started crying. If I went grocery shopping, I could be so exhausted for days afterwards that I couldn't bear to do anything but lie in bed. If I ran into an acquaintance at the store, I barely remembered it and absolutely could not remember what I had been talking about. After 12 o'clock every day, I started to feel like I was drunk. I started losing my balance and coordination and got dizzy. That's what life was like until I found UMS and started following the different steps in school. Then, within a few weeks, I started to feel the difference.

What made me realize that I had found something that could get me out of my illness was the Golden Milk! I started drinking the Golden Milk every night, and after many weeks I realized, I was starting to get my cognitive abilities back. It happened so fast that I could not believe it. The happiness when I noticed the change was unreal – I could read longer texts, remember them, and even reproduce them to relay a message to my husband. It was amazing.

So, I followed UMS the Fatigue school step-by-step for 9 months. Since the ingredients of Golden Milk are anti-inflammatory and brain fog is caused by inflammation in the brain, I was able to get my cognitive abilities back almost entirely. But my body was still tired, and I was limited by getting tired from physical activity. In my head, I was alert and had lots of joy, but life was still limited as my body could not cope.

The fact that it was difficult to recover on my own was since I had, among other things, a heavy metal poisoning and some deficiencies of various kinds. If you follow the UMS the Fatigue school method, course 3 teaches you that you can do an analysis to see if you have any deficiencies or if you have toxins in your body.

I decided to do an analysis and the result showed that I had sky-high values of uranium in my body along with high levels of beryllium. The nutritional deficiency was since my internal organs, liver, kidneys, adrenal glands, intestines, and hormonal system could no longer functioned as they should, and the body simply could not absorb nutrition's due to this.

The various organs of the body all work together to ensure you are healthy; if even one is affected, the rest of the system is affected in various ways. Because the internal organs were so burdened with toxins, I needed help detoxifying so that my body would have a chance to heal and function normally again. That's when I decided to go to India to detoxify.

After studying UMS, I realized that it is not surprising at all that so many people today suffer from Fatigue. Our body ends up absorbing everything that we eat, drink, breathe, and apply on our skin. Today, most of these contain toxins, chemicals, and endocrine disruptions that our body cannot purge. These disruptors are in the air, water, food, skin care products, cleaning products, medicines, and pesticides. The list is long. One of the sections in UMS will help you make sure that you start exchanging as much as you can for non-toxic alternatives. But when you have accumulated enough toxins for many years, it may be necessary to cleanse the body of these.

Now imagine that for a long time you have burdened the body with more toxins than it could get rid of. You may also live in an environment where there is mold, which puts even more strain on the body. Add to that that you live a life where there has been internal or external stress affecting you. Whether it's internal stress or external stress, it affects you both mentally and physically. There are too many straws that "break the camel's back".

The stress and toxins together quickly break you down and suddenly the Fatigue is a part of daily life. Unfortunately, many believe that it is the stress and only the stress that is the "culprit", that the Fatigue is mental and that you should be able to rest to get healthy, get lighter tasks at your workplace and that two months of sick leave should do the trick. But there are thousands of us who can attest that it is far, far from the truth of what will help a person with Fatigue heal and regain themselves. How many of us have blamed ourselves for not being able to change ourselves despite six months of sick leave? How many of us are who have despaired in our loneliness and wondered what is wrong with us? Why can't I get well, even though I'm struggling, even though I've tried so much to get fit again. Am I crazy, crazy, stupid? Will it always be like this, why just me, what have I done wrong?!

Had it been so simple that it was only because of stress, then all that rest and meditation would probably have helped. But it's hard, I'd say it's impossible, to rest to health after poisoning. Once you understand that, it's easier to no longer be so disappointed, despondent, and frustrated with yourself. Now you have gained an important insight and can start working for your recovery in a completely different way.

I spent three weeks in the Ayurvedic hospitals that UMS recommends. I will carry that experience with me for the rest of my life and my plan is to return at regular intervals for the rest of my life. That's where I got my life back. It's a tough step to take. You should follow the different methods of the school until you conclude that you need to go to India. You need to build yourself up to be able to make the journey, but even on the spot it is a purification of all: body, mind, and soul. It can be tough, but the staff takes incredible care of you. You should know that it's not a spa trip as some people think. But it's amazing.

I came back from India in mid-June 2017 and in October 2017 I got a full-time job at a workplace where I worked for four years.

Today, I have resigned for six months and have stated that, although I am not sick as I was in 2016 when I started school, full-time is not for me. Now, I follow my dream of working with what I am passionate about, which includes supporting others who live in Fatigue or have other challenges mentally or physically. If you're reading this, I want to congratulate you on finding your way here and encourage you to follow the school. This is your path to recovery. I promise. Should you read this text and not have Fatigue, you can still follow the school and you can still invest in yourself and your sustainable health for the future and go to India to the Ayurvedic hospitals.

Good luck!

The playlist[1] on YouTube contains two videos about what Kristina writes about.

---

[1] https://youtube.com/playlist?list=PLVmHtRW0bTN80a7nmvVAolK4YxZb 3QsCg

UMS collaborates with a hospital group of five facilities. The image below is of their smallest facility.

"Fatigue" is an alarm that goes off

Dr. Jared Younger: Innovative Research on Neuroinflar ⌃

In the playlist on YouTube, we meet professor and researcher Dr. Jared Younger, who studies the phenomena we discuss at UMS.

"Fatigue" is a symptom, and not a disease. Behind this symptom, various diseases and root causes can lie, often even more than one, which all have provoked inflammation in the brain. All of us who are now healthy have looked for these underlying illnesses and found the ones that affect us.

We've all started by reading the international symptom lists to see if we recognize the symptoms. We also use private labs in Sweden,

Germany, England, and the USA. A few members have received help at their health center, and a lab in London can test urine samples for heavy traces of lead.

It is as I wrote in the book "Mold poisoned" that mold toxins are not part of medical education in Sweden. The United States has long had the same problem and they've been fortunate to have Dr. Shoemaker, who is like a tiger on the issue, and he's created trainings for doctors. We'll discuss more about his findings later.

We have been operating for six years and have members who have found all sorts of poisonings; everything from mold, nickel, copper, aluminum and uranium and other metals to Lyme disease, twar and parasites. To get well, you must find your poisoning root and eliminate it. Until that happens, you generally just get sicker and sicker.

In Sweden, cases diagnosed as "chronic fatigue" or Fatigue are often treated as" mental illness", and patients are prescribed psychotropic drugs, therapy, and other suggestions that don't affect mold, parasites, or uranium.

I have never understood why foreign studies, research, experience, and knowledge never reached Sweden, even in the summer of 2016. Dr. Jarred Younger is a cutting-edge researcher on CFS, neuro inflammation, pain and fatigue syndrome, and there are many others in his field with immense knowledge on the topic. In

March 2022, a magazine for doctors published an article titled "Brain fatigue - an invisible scourge", and if you read it, you will see that the distance between domestic and international knowledge is abysmal.

For example, they consider the cause of brain fog to be completely unknown. So, residents of Sweden are forced to turn abroad if we want to get healthy.

The UMS method is an import. I got well from these methods and am, so to speak, UMS the Fatigue school member number one. I brought home the methods, which made me healthy, and now we have many who have followed in my footsteps and who are already recovered or on the path to health as well.

I consider that I was fully recovered by March 2016. Before this point, I had experienced the worst of fatigue and brain fog – I knew what it was like to wake up paralyzed, not be able to remember my children's names, not been capable of simple tasks. I was a risk to myself and my surroundings; my car had once ended up in a small ditch because I had forgotten to tighten the handbrake in Coop's parking lot!

I was considered to have worked too much and shut down my businesses of my three healthy companies, completely unnecessarily. We have members who have been asked for a divorce!

Symptom map

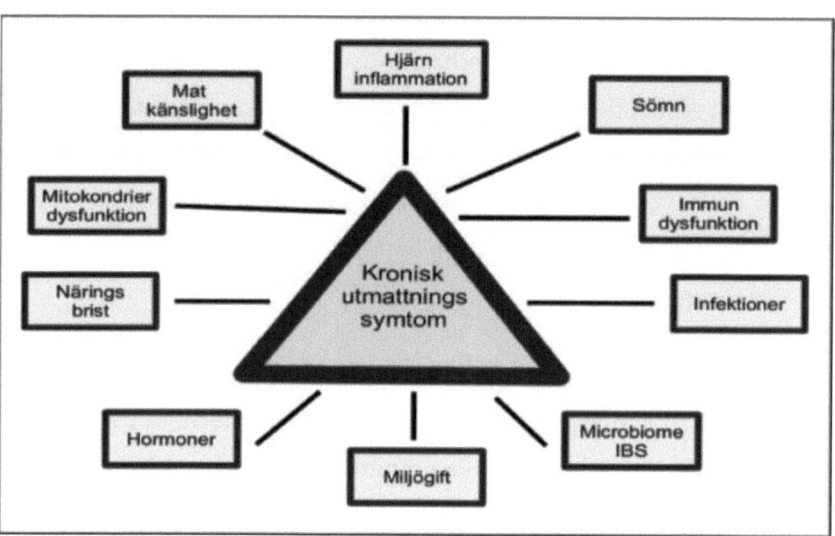

This is the symptom map, around which the entire UMS method has been built. At the top we see the symptom "brain inflammation", which is tackled in course one using Golden Milk and other methods to reduce inflammation.

Then comes course 2, which focuses on sleep. This includes a clean sleeping environment, so we sanitize the bedroom among many other things.

Most people find course 2 very fun, because they are finally rid of brain fog and are starting to get better.

Carina, fell ill in 2014

Carina has completed the program. She was a part of a UMS veteran ground that was for people who had been on long-term sick leave, so called" hopeless cases".

Hello Lena!

I fell ill in February '14 and had been very ill. But thanks to the Umattnings-skolan.se, I have now been healthy for about 13 months. I joined the school at the very beginning. I haven't done all the courses, as I have just gotten to course 8. But I can't remember the last time when I felt as good as I do now. At the beginning of this year, I started my third year in college. A few years ago, I would have thought this impossible. But I am getting my life back on track and it feels great! I really want to thank you for helping me and many others get their lives back, or even getting a better life, by sharing your knowledge and experience.

Thank you, Carina Frogner

Carina has also communicated the same thing to her fellow students. One of the strengths of UMS the Fatigue school is the Facebook groups that act as self-help groups. Since it is impossible for me to personally answer to hundreds of people, this allows them to help each other in general cases and reach out to me in emergency.

In April 2022, Carina wrote:

I never did any analysis but in retrospect I have understood that I have had long-term fluid deficiency, Candida, and copper poisoning (due to a copper IUD) all of which were exacerbated by large intake of diet soda, chemical hair dye and gluten intolerance.

Physical, not mental causes

What happens to everyone who starts in the School of Fatigue or encounters my texts, is that they begin to slowly let go of the idea that everything is social, psychological, or work-related. In course 1 and 2, we work on being able to stand on your feet and get rid of the brain fog you get from inflammation.

When I fell ill in Sweden, was asked by a physiotherapist to walk with crutches as fast as I could it led to a completely indescribable dizziness and did not help at all. Then I sought and received care and cure abroad, and one of the first things doctors told me was: Sit still! Don't move! You have a severe inflammation of the hippocampus!

But the most chilling statement, which I heard after I sought medical care in India, was made by my company doctor: Good! I don't know how they do, but I've seen many come back healthy from there!

There are more members who have reported that their doctors consider it brilliant that they are doing the UMS method.

I've collected some texts in the multi translatable UMS domain www.utmattad.net also about conversations that members have had with their doctors.

We start looking for the root cause in course 3

"When did I get sick? Had I brought something new into my environment then?"

This is one of the first questions to ask, even if the patient thinks that they have been poisoned as children. Of course, it is possible that it is from ingesting toxic paint at an artists' home or by playing with tin soldiers all the time. But often, something changed in the environment when the Fatigue first started.

We had a woman who had been completely exhausted for many, many years. When we asked her this question, she figured that she had acquired a special sterilization method – Essure – as a contraceptive. She then began to seek information about what it was that they had really put in her.

I gave her links at the start, and then she looked up symptom lists and recognized just about everything. She concluded that the product contained nickel and she was allergic to it. Then she had the health care to remove everything and of course the brain fog cleared immediately. But, as she herself told me, she went through the entire school to heal the consequences of the fatigue.

This particular "exhausted" woman was given antidepressant medication, and often if you don't eat psychotropic drugs, you don't get sick leave. It is a kind of forced medication that is prohibited by Swedish law. It also does not cure inflamed brains or nickel poisonings.

But if it is considered that Fatigue can only be because one's family, one's social life, one's psyche, or work, thousands and thousands of women will be regularly abused

Carola, still healthy?

April 2022: I feel great now, working full time, I eat good whole foods and I have enough energy for leisure as well.

I am enormously grateful to you Lena and UMS for giving me my life back.

My diet is low carb/keto, leaving out fast carbs since they were probably the last root cause of my exhaustion/depression.

As soon as I eat potatoes, rice or gluten-free pasta and gluten-free bread (aka starchy carbs) I get so tired, and the brain fog kicks in (I haven't eaten white sugar at all since I started UMS). My diet is now clean low carb/keto made from whole foods without additives and with healthy good fats. I always feel refreshed, and I have a lot of energy. I turned 55 recently but I feel like I am 30 again.

One of the symptoms of brain fog for me is food hypersensitivity, every person is different. One may be sensitive to white bread and the other to milk. I asked Carola about her disease roots. "Only when I had started the UMS parasite course doing parasite cleanse, I felt great improvement in just a couple of weeks, and I felt completely restored after the parasite cleanse.

After this I experienced that I still could improve my health even more. Before the parasite cleanse, I reduced the amount of plastic and aluminum in my household (mainly plastic cans for food storage and the Teflon frying pan, as I didn't use any deodorant), and I had been on a gluten free diet for years before this (I don't have celiac disease, but I got a stomachache from gluten and my doctor thinks this is food sensitivity). Sugar was never good for me, but I still consumed sugar before UMS as it gave me some comfort.

I had quite a few toxic relationships in my life (especially one of my so-called close friends) that I needed to remove from my surroundings.

When my physical wellbeing increased, I was psychologically able to take the fights with these people who "stole" my energy and then being able to manage the stress of saying NO when I wanted to say NO., I was a huge people pleaser back then. Now I have no problem with such things anymore.

So, to my root's causes. I start with the most crucial ones: parasites, gluten, sugar, toxic relationships, e-substances, fast carbohydrates (too much fruit also gives me brain fog), aluminum, large amounts of dairy products do not suit me either, I use a little sometimes if I need to in my cooking, but it is always best for me to leave dairy out of my diet. I had a leaky gut problem and I have healed it with UMS bone broth.

I certainly had some serious nutritional deficiencies back then. I was exhausted for over two years before UMS, but on a sick leave for about six months before UMS with the doctor's words ringing in my ears: "Since it is now the third long sick leave due to exhaustion/severe depression, you will most likely never be fully recovered again. My doctor suggested: "We have to think about part-time disability pension for You". I was classified as forever "ruined" by the exhaustion/depression.

To this day, my doctor raises her eyebrows at check up every year and give all credit for my well-being to "good medication" for thyroid dysfunction and my Addison's disease (adrenal insufficiency) as my adrenals are completely shut down since over 20 years ago. My doctor does not think my lifestyle change has anything to do with me being in such a good health nowadays which surprises me a lot.

With a whole food diet, I have been able to reduce both my medications by 25% to this day. The healing continues although I am completely recovered from exhaustion/brain fog and depression.

Before starting UMS, I had two long periods of sick leave in 6-7 years. Now I have been working as a full-time nurse for over four years in a physically and mentally challenging unit and I am doing incredibly well. I am now having new challenges at work since changing my work position and I am about to start working in a palliative care unit. I do have the energy to challenge myself with new surroundings and I am thriving.

I dare to dream again about my future and setting new goals. This tells me that I am now healthy, and I do have the energy to enjoy my spare time with new hobbies as well.

Symptoms double down quickly

Our experience is that it starts with one or two of the major symptom pieces, and then onions are put on the salmon all the time until a ME/CFS diagnosis; Myalgic Encephalomyelitis/Chronic Fatigue Syndrome.

For a ME/CFS diagnosis, the patient must meet all the criteria, which are called the "Canada criteria". It is considered incurable because the treatments they use, such as talk therapy, do not affect toxins and mold.

The diagnosis therefore becomes a manslaughter blow.

1. Exercise-induced deterioration and Fatigue
2. Sleep disturbance
3. Pain
4. Two or more neurological/cognitive symptoms
5. One or more symptoms from two of the categories of autonomic, neuroendocrine, or immunological manifestations
6. Symptoms have persisted for at least 6 months

7.

In June 2018, Marita wrote:

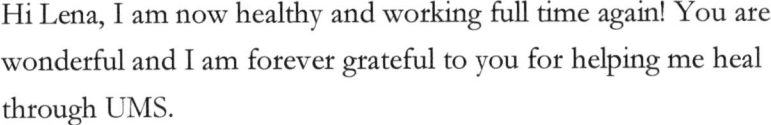

Hi Lena, I am now healthy and working full time again! You are wonderful and I am forever grateful to you for helping me heal through UMS.

I don't know what my root was, but I am convinced that I stressed my way to imbalances in the body and then did not have resistance to what it may have been some heavy metals, parasites, or leaky gut. I just know that I was suffering from fog brains, my brain felt overheated, and every single cell in my body felt like it was shaking. I couldn't think clearly, both long-term and short-term memory were poor, and body aches, powerlessness and listlessness were common.

I was helped by the school Golden Milk, the elevator*, lemon water, ginger etcetera. I had high blood sugar, sleep apnea, was overweight and ate Levaxin for the thyroid gland. The doctor said I would have to take Levaxin for the rest of my life, but in March all the blood samples were taken again, and everything was fine including the thyroid gland; I haven't taken Levaxin for 11 months! Blood sugar is good, I no longer suffer sleep apnea and I lost 10 pounds. Needless to say, I feel amazingly good! It's a wonderful feeling! 💜

Thank you, Lena, without your involvement with the school I wouldn't have felt this good today!

I got well in 1.5 years through the help of the school. It's a hell of a fatigue syndrome!

I suffered Fatigue for the first time in 2000 and was on sick leave for six years, then a short toss sick leave of 2 months in 2015 and then in 2017 I was on sick leave for one year.

I've never really been healthy since the first time but now it's completely different and I've gotten to know my body and I know what I need.

I've had a stressful period now since I went up to full-time work, but instead of stressed, I feel calm inside, weird! Of course, I am tired after my work, but a normal fatigue, not exhausted!

Hugs from,
Marita Ahlgren

* The "Elevator" is a drink UMS uses for those who have cortisol problems.

I asked, in April '22, how Marita is feeling:

I still work full time and will retire this next year when I turn 65, but the plan is for it to be part-time as I think it's so fun to work! I am so grateful for UMS as it really changed my life!

I took two trips to India, and I wouldn't have gotten that help without your help and UMS.

Kind regards
Marita Ahlgren

What do the problems look like?

I have been ill, diagnosed "Fatigue", and I considered to be over-worked. I became so small in early 2010, and the advice I was given was to work less, exercise more and take some sleeping pills. Of course, it did not work.

Those who suffer from Fatigue often pant, which is why it is believed that we are in poor condition.

This depends on the PH value, and in school the topic is covered in courses 1 and 2. In Sweden, the PH value problem "does not exist". It is probably this archetypic panting that makes those around us think that we should exercise. We get much sicker in this phase by moving.

In the video playlist there are videos about the matter.

We can't run up a flight of stairs without panting. Some feel that they barely get air in the afternoon or evening. They apparently misinterpret it in Sweden and think that it is asthma, smoking or poor fitness. Balance the PH and it will disappear! Out with junk food, and in with real food. Pears are also an excellent help for the lungs ,as well as licorice root powder and it's fifteen seedlings.

Three minutes of stress requires two days of recovery for someone who is suffering Fatigue. I quite often see Swedes who regard The Cypriots as "lazy".

They miss burned out in Cyprus... where I now live full time since 2014, commuted a couple of years before. The pace in Sweden is morbidly high, and one of the things "all" Swedes abroad react to when visiting. Plus, everyone should do everything themselves which is why service is completely lacking.

As a sick person, it's important to learn to breathe correctly, and in the playlist on YouTube there are videos about the matter. However, you should be over course 3 before you start moving, for example, via Yoga. It is quite enough to breathe for the one who is poisoned, movement can come later.

The UMS program is all about detoxifying widely as well as building immune system at the same time. It takes 2.5 - 3 years to fully recover, and you can get a significant help along the way by visiting Indian doctors during course 3.

If you can't or don't want to, you can get the same result via UMS the Fatigue school, but it takes longer. We cannot use their methods because they require a trained doctor present. When you get home, you can basically skip courses 3 to 7, and head to course.

In March 2017, the collaboration began in earnest.

The doctor in the video titled "7 Fatigue Recovery Mistakes," which is in the playlist, goes over the seven mistakes that one makes in the West, and the symptoms that this cause.

As common culprits, he points out too many drugs, bad doctors who can't diagnose properly but who guess wildly, medications that are prescribed such as sleeping pills and psychotropic drugs that make the symptoms much worse instead of focusing on the root.

No one sees big picture!

The doctor also describes not understanding the connections between the organs involved. Western doctors have an overconfidence in blood tests, and we already know that they often show completely wrong results regarding, for example, cortisol. Finally, he believes that there is a lack of programs to get well.

This is exactly what the School of Fatigue wants to give affected comrades, and I have therefore created a nine-episode action plan[2], which is a bit Swedish, but approved by the doctors I work with. Sick leave is only increasing and increasing, and you don't understand why. The doctors we use explain quite well why, and people really suffer unnecessarily.

"So changes the brain during burnout"[3] is a decent article because they mention the stress hormone cortisol as the culprit. Then the ideas held by medical professionals in Sweden is the truth.

In 2011–12, nothing was known, and many doctors have been caught up in the fact that it is probably "psychological" (hence all talk therapy and psychotropic drugs).

The researcher also says: *"Today there is no consensus on exactly how burnout should be treated, although it is known that team rehabilitation and work-oriented rehabilitation, among other things, can make people better. Methods used include relaxation exercises, cognitive behavioral therapy, sleep school and coaching."*

Many students at UMS also tell us that they are given psychotropic drugs, therapies, forced to work out, walk with crutches, etc. We can state that there is no cure at all in Sweden, which is backed by the research conducted.

---

[2] https://utmattningsskolan.se/kursoversikt/

[3] https://utmattningsskolan.se/wp-content/uploads/2022/06/How-the-brain-changes-with-burnout-Motivation.se-Motivation.pdf

And because you can't cure in depth, people relapse, and then it gets worse," says the researcher. *"That's the worst thing about this – those who have once been burned out carry with them a vulnerability and very easily get bad again. If this happens, there is a risk that they will collapse completely. So, the prognosis is unfortunately quite poor, therefore it is important to proceed cautiously and not be in too much of a hurry back to work. In many cases, a change of workplace is necessary.*

There is penance – abroad, and the School of Attrition has brought it home.

Mia's story is common

Thank you, Lena, for your Fatigue school that gave me my life back. I am now eating right, drinking right, sleeping – thinking about what's important in life and learning how to set boundaries.

What is Fatigue? Well, it is to fall into a big dark hole with no rescue. For me, the Fatigue after twenty years came with completely unacceptable stress as a single mother to two wonderful boys with absent fathers who did the most to destroy but never met their sons. Having been brought up to be a good girl, who was never allowed to give up, I fought on; full-time jobs, children, houses, old parents, social life...

The stress causes the body to break, and, in my case, it led to a long and tough struggle, and when I got a severe bronchitis and lost sleep then the whole brain broke. Just as Lena often writes, my brain became inflamed in connection with a cold, and it was then broken for years, sending out strange signals, anxiety and totally screwed up thoughts.

I had a constant headache at the highest level around the clock for two years until I had been detoxified via UMS ' first four courses, and I chose to go down to India was helped with my recovery there. If you don't want to or can't go down, you take the last UMS courses 5-9 for the same result, but it takes longer. In the hospital, they can detoxify faster than you can do at home.

I turned to our health care system first, but they have no knowledge regarding Fatigue, especially when it has gotten so bad. I hardly believe that I managed to survive, after two years in bed and another two years of healing, I now work 100% again and feel restored to 95%.

If your health care center fails to make you healthy on sleeping pills and antidepressants, you are quickly transferred to psychiatry where they tamper with your life. You get medicine after medicine; insertion and withdrawal, and no support when the antidepressants give you suicidal thoughts. You get to try psychosis medicine, bipolar medicine, sleeping pills, benzos, and there's no stopping, and suddenly, you're a legal junkie. Our doctors have no plan how to get rid of these, but you will be drugged for the rest of your life?!? I bring with me a trauma from the health care system that I am learning process and every year it gets better.

I was so bad in my Fatigue my brain felt broken, I couldn't read, I couldn't understand, and I struggled day and night to get well again. My Fatigue had nothing to do with mental illness but that's how I was treated from being a healthy fully working single mother of two to being considered the bottom scrape of society.

I went in and out of psychiatric wards, I think I spent four or five visits there for 3-4 weeks each time. I had to put myself in, so that I wouldn't kill myself, with those horrible suicidal thoughts that the prescribed psych medicine itself provokes! I tried electric shocks in three rounds and some other method called TMS and I just felt like I was living in the movie "Cuckoo's Nest".

I wrote farewell letters to my kids, to family and friends and I really thought it was the end for me.

I started with Lena's Fatigue school and at first, I was too sick to keep up, but struggled on, and after two years in school I got support and help to get to India. That possibility opens in course 3, before that there is no point in trying to go to India.

The Ayurvedic hospital in India was salvation for me, with the right diets, treatments, yoga, care, and love. I began to heal during the 23 days that I was there. I got a lot healthier and continued to do what I was taught when I came back to Sweden. I got so good that in August of the same year I went down once more and stayed for another 23 days.

They succeeded in their way of looking at the body as a whole, getting me to heal and come back. Then it became a long process to heal all the trauma that I had been subjected to in mainstream medical care.

Many people think that we exhausted have weak nerves, while we are probably the strongest, who never give up, even when the body crashes.

Thanks again Lena.
Hugs, Mia

Mold is very common as a root

I have a specific book dedicated to those who have suffered mold poisoning, entitled "Mold poisoned". If the symptom list is not surety enough or a specific diagnosis is required, we collect urine samples to send to England to test for mold. That book also has its own website, and you should start by reading through the symptom list; anyone who has mold poisoning should find a description of their problems in the symptom list.

When the hippocampus is inflamed, it sends out and receives signals completely wrong.

I woke up one morning and couldn't move. My muscles didn't care what I wanted. Even though I told my brain to tell my legs to move. Abruptly silent. Nothing happened.

In Sweden, the disease is work-related, mental, social and doesn't even really "exist" that it is an inflammation of the brain. We ourselves often agree with it at the beginning; must be the stress at work! It's stressful to even be Swedish! Had a difficult divorce! Crisis in the company! Was the victim of a robbery!

Researchers in Sweden have established that no one, absolutely no one, has been cured in the kingdom. That's because you never cure the inflammation, nor do you ever dig up what causes it.

We do it in school, and take every word, every lesson bloody seriously because you could easily end up paralyzed.

I just shut down all the business, poof! I couldn't take care of it anyway. The ability to count had completely ceased. I destroyed 20-year-old companies in a flash.

Example: I would pay a large amount of money from one company to another - pay a debt - and when I made the transfer, I had doubled the debt because I had thought wrong. I paid bills constantly three times, or not at all. I forgot promises, didn't remember people's names, barely recognized people, didn't remember my daughter's first name.

Marie Gadd has got her life back

I've been around since you started school. Or rather, it was just a couple of days old.

To the left is a photo from the fall of 2017, and to the right is one taken in July 2019. I was suffering Fatigue since 2011 and now I'm going out soon to work! Much thanks to you, who have opened my eyes when it comes to food, spices and herbs.

My copper poisoning is better, the hefty nutritional deficiency I've had and the dangerous inflammation are almost completely gone. The parasites will soon be eliminated. My incipient diabetes has backed off. The "chronic" inflammation of the right elbow and the pain in the right knee are 95% better. Soon gone, that is.

I've worked in mold damaged workplaces, so this is another root I've started working on. Vitamin B12 deficiency and low vitamin D are also two areas I am working on right now. When I've got rid of mold in me, and gotten my B12 and D level up, I hope I'm healthy.

I still drink the golden milk at times when the brain lags behind and the pressure comes back in my head. I avoid gluten, meat, and sugar. It takes time to get healthy and I have a long way to go but how glorious life is now that I can enjoy it again. Many thanks for being there! "

I asked Marie in April 2022 how things are nowadays, and told her that I'm going to produce this give-up-book:

"I hope it can be useful to others. I was on sick leave 100% since 2011. Now I've been working 25% since just over two years, and feel much better compared to 2015 which was the worst where I didn't even remember my own name.

Recovery is progressing but slowly. The great positive of having been completely lost in Fatigue is the immense happiness and gratitude I feel every day for the progress that has taken place and is still happening."

I asked Sofia Stark the same thing

 "It's going great. I don't really remember the years of illness but I was completely on sick leave all of 2013.

Now I work full time, and have a creative hobby business, making things in wool and making candles. I take care of 20 sheep and 17 lambs, a border collie and two cats as well as my two daughters, my own villa and a special resident. I think life works now. Although, of course, I still have a headache, worse memory and have to sleep through dinner sometimes.

I could add that I feel better if I take care of myself dietarily; eat good food and don't drink alcohol." Sofia's root was fluoride and radon in the water. There are quite a few now who are through the UMS program, and they are completely healthy, and Sofia was the one who first announced results in November 2016. I started UMS at the end of July of that year. In the picture, at least, I see that she was as poisoned as anyone can even get; no pupils, and you can barely see her eyeballs.

We have our own doctors via Skype

The school of Fatigue has an agreement with a hospital, the best, and which I have investigated carefully and visited twice.

In course 1 to 3, you are prepared for the detoxification and start undergoing a broad detoxification. In course 3, you get access via Skype to these detoxification specialists.

Although you can complete the course by yourself at home, you can get so much more out of the time in the hospital. Once you have covered courses 1 to 3, you will be able to cope with a trip even if you require assistance. We have a rule that you can only go once you have completed courses 1 and 2 after two members with severe brain fog went to the hospital directly in course 1. Of course, since they had not successfully reduced the brain inflammation, the treatments did not work for them. Now, with the rule in place, all members can get the most out of their visit.

To begin the process, you first email your test results and symptom lists to the given address. Once they receive your email, one of their 20 certified doctors calls you and the call lasts for about half an hour. During this call, the doctor pays close attention to the patient's symptom list. We have found that medical arrogance is absent in Indian culture; the doctor has the attitude that sick people should have all the attention and all the help they can get because they are powerless without it.

Since the School of Fatigue is a non-profit service[4], I had to set the price myself. I set the price at SEK 200: - per consultation. After the Skype call, the patient receives a diet and Indian medicine list. The school also has its own schoolyard – divided into specific FB groups – one for those who want to hire the doctors, and one for those who have been there.

---

[4] https://utmattningsskolan.se/2017/03/28/skolans-prispolitik/

Can we guarantee
that you will be healthy?

In the school there are many individuals, and those who heavy metal or mold poisoning can cope with routinely utilizing the hospital as well as the UMS program. At home, we start the process of cleaning out the foreign components in our body. The doctors in India do the same; they clean all the organs and then drive out any substances that should not be there.

Like UMS, they detoxify and build the immune systems at the same time. However, since there is medical supervision, they can use completely different "heavier" purging foods as well as lots of body treatments to do the process quickly.

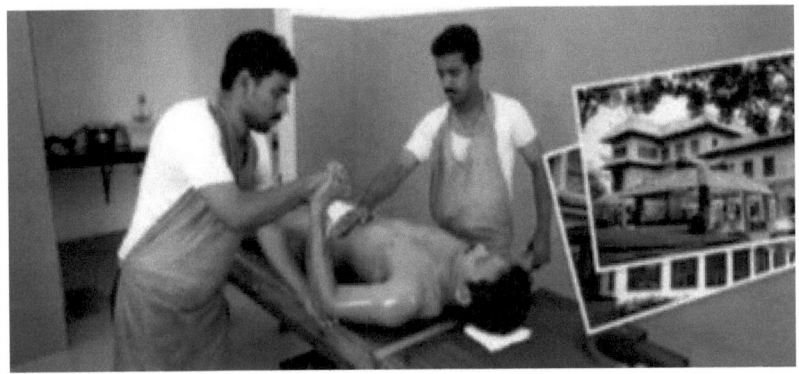

At UMS, we use a lighter artillery, which does not require medical supervision, to detoxify the organs and mainly the liver. We have already spoken about Golden Milk and the Elevator, but all detoxifying agents are equally important.

We cannot promise everyone that they will be healed, but there is great hope, and it has been proven many times since the conception of this school.

We have done surveys and kept track of members so to ensure that they were truly getting benefits from the programs of the school.

Kerala has many
health tourism facilities

When I was hospitalized for five weeks myself, I saw with my own eyes how "Western wrecks" came in and were discharged five weeks later looking 20 years younger. I underwent this "rejuvenation".

Fear venoms produce a lot of "hard" wrinkles, and we learn in course 3 how to track certain poisonings just by studying one's face. These wrinkles are mistakenly interpreted by us as signs of aging. At one point in my sickness, I looked 75 years old, and I experienced first-hand the shock that the people around me felt when I healed. We have plenty of members who have reported that co-workers, relatives, and friends who haven't seen them in a year react quite positively they see the results of the detoxification.

Copper poisoning is particularly tricky; those affected by it get so stressed that they can hardly sit still. So many people are affected by copper poisoning that it may be the reason why Fatigue is often attributed to "stress".

Many members have also been under pressure and stress from our authorities and health care system who want them to get well as quickly as possible. The government is apparently annoyed that this group never gets well. Of course, they can't heal without detoxification, and so I went down to India and made an agreement with the hospital director. The school members raised money for that trip, for which I was very grateful for, but we all felt that I had to go down and talk to them on the spot, see the patients myself, ask tricky questions I already knew the answers to ask around the resort, and ask professionals in India to check them out.

Our members have gone to doctors in Sweden, but they are tied up, and can do nothing, Moment 22.

Heavy metal poisonings "do not exist" in Sweden and doctors are not trained to identify or cure them; therefore, they can also do nothing more than prescribe antidepressants, which do not help. Due to this, poisoned people rarely ever get better in Sweden, and tougher measures are being taken for it, none of which include detoxification. This will not help, it will only serve to torment many, and I fear that suicides will increase.

As a poisoned person, it is easy to lose hope when the system is not designed to help you. When the "cures" you are prescribed generally only make you sicker, you become desperate to find a way out. I can't consider it anything other than foolish to think that you can cure poisonings with "tougher measures" that don't include detoxifying.

Especially since it is quite easily to get rid of aluminum poisoning, which is something I suffered from. Since aluminum (and uranium) have been found in the Swedish rainwater, we detoxify aluminum widely and collectively in course 3.

The school's method is very effective, but it can take time, so those who are still sick in the last step of course 3 can now get their own private doctor to help them detoxify. Some of the doctors are Indians, but I also met a trained chemical medic from Ireland as well as one from Canada, who switched over and was now working with Ayurveda.

The school of Fatigue is really nothing more than an attempt, which has worked out well, to mimic my own recovery.

A spouse speaks out

In February 2020, a 37-year-old man chose to take his own life. From the article below, you can read that he had a really hard time, and by all accounts he took his own life because he had tried everything and did not think he had any hope in treating his ME/CFS.

At the same time, not even 50 km from us, and there is Petrea.

In 2016, Petrea had had ME/CFS (according to the Canada concensus criteria) since the year 2001. She had been suffering for 15 years when she received her sentence from the health care system: she would never be able to get back to work. Of course, the doctor did not want her to lose all hope, so he said that she may be able to come back 25%, but he did not truly believe it,

Petrea faced the undeniable truth – there is no solution worth being called a treatment for ME/CFS sufferers in Region Dalarna. So Petrea had to look up a treatment herself, started the School of Fatigue, and after that treatment she has got her life back. She doesn't have ME/CFS (according to The Canada concensus criteria) anymore. Now she is back and has chosen to work part-time 50-75% and currently studies full time.

But Petrea has had to find the treatment herself and bear all the costs personal as Region Dalarna does not provide the care needed.

I am not trying to say that the School of Fatigue is the solution for all people who have ME/CFS; I know well enough that it is a difficult disease to cure, but I know one person who has gotten their life back – Petrea.

THAT is evidence to me, and this NO ONE will be able to take our life away from us!

Håkan Marklund

It has become the fashion to eat supplements

The last time I was in India, the doctors mentioned that they have met many people from the West who are poisoned by supplements. I was aware of this, and UMS uses the food route instead of the supplements available as pills.

I remember that a member once mentioned that a Swedish doctor told him that turmeric capsules can damage your liver. Yes, in the capsules UMS advises against, turmeric pills are one of them. We choose the food route instead, real turmeric root.

Anyone who suffers from stress, worry, anxiety, is exhausted and so on would do well to study the liver knowledge that is inside the school or ask a relative to do so. The video playlist that belongs to this book also has a portion about just the liver.

Unfortunately, we must go abroad, because in Sweden "elevated liver values" are mainly associated with drinking too much alcohol. In the image below, you see a portion of the video you can find in the book's playlist on YouTube, that names mold, which is a common root of Fatigue.

Reality:

104 out of 112 (93%) of ME/CFS patients had mycotoxins in their urine compared to 0% in a healthy control group. [5]

"We are seeing clear evidence that ME is a bodily disease, with abnormalities in both metabolism and in the immune system," says Anders Rosén, professor emeritus of cell biology at Linköping University. This means that Swedish researchers have finally figured out that CFS and ME are physical diseases - but they have not linked it with mold - as the United States has already done, along with several other countries.

Unfortunately, since Swedish research has not reached this place, the research available to us is either not written in Swedish or is not good enough, and then the problem is swept under the rug – it "does not exist".

[5] https://www.ncbi.nlm.nih.gov/pmc/articles/PMC3705282/

This is even though the National Institute of Public Health has indicated that they believe that 1.7 million Swedes are sick due to mold housing.

In the playlist on YouTube, you will find "Dr. Ritchie Shoemaker - on mold" and he is behind the fact that the United States is far ahead of us.

In the early 2000s,
they were one million

The houses that make one million Swedes sick, it says on the
leaflet.

Government Department for wanted a breakdown misnomer, I
describe it in the book "Mold poisoned", but the Prime Minister
was not interested.

My experience after six years is that mold is then most common
causes of "Fatigue". The list of symptoms for Fatigue in Sweden
greatly overlap with the international list for mold poisoning.

International Symptom List

Decreased ability to concentrate (brain fog), depression, stomach pain, aches, personality changes, mood swings, increased anxiety and panic reactions, lethargy and apathy, aggression, impaired short memory, (brain fog), worry, bleeding gums, bleeding in the brain, bleeding tendency, blood that does not coagulate, blurred vision and visual disturbances, bone marrow disorders, burning sensation in the mouth, chest, chronic fatigue, recurrent infections and flu pain, decreased sensory acuity, coma, confusion, cough, skin crawls, damage to the heart, diarrhea, difficulty breathing, difficulty concentrating, increased tendency to alcohol, sugar and cigarette addiction, slower reflexes and more difficulty speaking, disorientation, dizziness, drowsiness, eye damage, eye inflammation, fever, hair loss, hallucinations, headache, hearing loss, inflammation of the heart, internal bleeding, impaired immune system, itchy nose, jaundice, joint pain, stiffness in joints, decreased sex drive, liver diseases, low blood pressure, memory loss and memory problems, muscle pain, nausea, nosebleeds, numbness, pulmonary edema, red eyes, runny nose, seizures, tremors, impaired reflexes, sore throat, vomiting, vomiting blood, weakness, weight loss, wheezing and stressed behavior.

Sick leave for six years

In March 2018, Jeanette wrote:

"I want to convey hope to anyone new who is wondering whether or not the school works.

I joined the School of Fatiguein early August 2016, and have followed the school's courses with utmost attention to detail detail, with my inner feeling as a guide, and my loved ones as help and support."

She described her first memory of thinking: "wow, the course works"

It was a normal day when I had three tasks written on a note. As a sick person, I usually came home and realized that I had forgotten to do two of the tasks on the list.

Today was different though, as I was crossing the ISA parking lot after shopping, a thought popped into my head:

- Yes, I need to go to the library and get a book.

Where did that idea come from? How could I remember that? Normally I would have too much brain fog after shopping to remember anything.

I got rid of the brain fog in just a couple weeks, did a toxic analysis in course 3 and got the answer from the USA in November '16.

After I had received the analyses , I changed my diet to paleo and I have gotten rid of all the stomach problems such as hypersensitivity to, among other things, garlic.

Jeanette in April 2022

The journey of Fatigue in my case began in February 2010. I was immediately given antidepressant medication even after I conveyed that I didn't feel depressed, but more tired and exhausted. Cognitive behavioural therapy, physical movement, and depression courses came as suggestions later. During my period of sick leave, the health care system has been hesitant that the Swedish Social Insurance Agency would approve the sick leave if I turned down antidepressant medication and depression courses. Attending the depression courses, I felt left out. I've never felt the depression that my classmates had experienced.

When we don't understand why or who we're sick, we trust the doctors to give us the right advice to get well. If you are sick, your only desire is to get well.

My sick leave period was 6.5 years, and the health care recommend-dations have led to deterioration in my health all along the way.

I started out as a tired and worked out person and, just before I found UMS, I was pretty much bedridden around the clock with severe brain fatigue, so-called brain fog, sweating at the slightest exertion and sensitivity to light.

During the course of my Fatigue, a lot has happened that has stressed me, for example that the doctors would not write a medical certificate that the Social Insurance Agency approves and struggling with self-esteem in society where Fatigue is seen as a mental weakness. I tried to work but the employer ended up getting an ultimatum; we've done it all, resign or we'll terminate you. I have also met two doctors who told me that I suffered a brain injury from my Fatigue. "Work in special action about 25%" was what I could look forward to.

I found UMS by chance on Facebook in the fall of 2016 and I'm incredibly grateful for that. Once I found it, I followed the courses thoroughly.

I first through that my throat infection was a root cause, but after trying all the suggestions, I realized it was just the symptom of an inflamed organ. I read the symptoms list and studied hard, concluding that my gut must be inflamed, but it was not so.

Now, I know exactly what made me sick: a hormonal IUD was the root, exacerbated by a stressful job and many tough emotional events. This created an imbalance in my body. Once the hormonal IUD was withdrawn, it took about three weeks before I felt everything getting lighter in my body. I was back on track! After the first period since the withdrawal of the hormonal IUD, I got an obvious feeling that "now I am healthy". I remember when I first put on my sneakers that had been in the cupboard for three years and went for a 20-minute walk. It worked!

On the same day, I attended a meeting with the Swedish Public Employment Service where I managed to have a conversation with two people. I could keep up with them throughout the conversation! When I got home, I put on my sneakers again, and went for a 20-minute walk.

I had so many activities in the same day, and I had no heaviness, no inflammation, and no soreness in the throat. I was healthy! Absolutely wonderful!

In July 2016, I had all the criteria of severe ME/CFS. After about nine months with UMS, all the malaise in the body was gone.

Good luck finding your roots with the help of UMS!

Jeanette's mother

When Jeanette was through UMS, her mother wrote:

Hello Lena!

As I've already written, I've followed your school but only from the side-lines. I haven't enrolled but I've been following it because my daughter has been enrolled. She has been very ill for several years, but your help she has now been well for nine months… without any prescription medication. By following your school, putting the right things in her body, reading the homework and absorbing what she has read, she is now healthy.

[...]

It's absolutely amazing! Many thanks to you!! I sincerely wish you all the best, and I hope that you succeed in the task you have taken on. During these months, I have felt that it has been the right path, a natural way to take care of yourself and your body. I follow you with great interest.

[...]

Good luck with the continuation!

Regards NN

How is it now?

I asked that question six years later to the same mother:

"I am enormously happy and grateful that we have our daughter back. It's incredibly fun and nice after several lost years. I'm glad that she can be involved and that she is back in work. Life is starting to get normal again.

Had she not found the School of Fatigue, I'm not sure we'd still have her. She was in very bad shape, I remember I saw an old lady coming down the road slowly and tentatively, a little curled up. It was my own daughter at 39 years old!!! It was a terrible shock!

She's strong. She wanted to keep living, she had two children to take care of. In my eyes, she was incredibly good at being able to read and absorb what she needed to get well. It was a fight she won. She's still around today taking care of herself and her family and she's back in work.

After being away for years both privately and socially, it is not easy to return. The rest of us find it all too easy to judge and reject without having a clue what is behind it. It costs an enormous amount of energy to come again and become an ordinary member of society again.

I remember clearly, when my boss stepped forward and explained what responsibility the employer has when an employee for some reason can't be bothered to be at work. Admittedly, it's many years ago but it should still be what should apply, but that's not the case. My daughter's employer was a municipality! My daughter was forced to resign. She denied but was then told, if you don't do it yourself then we will do it and you will end up in a worse situation. But when you're healthy, you're welcome back.

The return was not easy. There were many applications to the municipality where she would be welcome back, all with negative responses. She has a successful education and previously fine grades. In the end, however, the solution came, so today there are jobs for her in the municipality as well.

Our experience shows that you should not give up, but of course it would be easier and less painful if we had a care that sees the whole person and listens to their patient. If we had a society where the knowledge exists that Fatigue has physical causes and is not about mental health problems. "

Jeanette's mother points to a phenomenon that I experienced, namely the reactions of those around me when I have been forced to quit my businesses or withdraw from usual life. There were really a few who even asked how I was feeling or even cared. At this point, the Asians' behavior towards the sick becomes a positive culture clash. On the other hand, we have members who have been scolded by Swedish medical professionals for not getting well.

Monika is now healthy

My time with UMS began when I enrolled in school in 2017. But

at the time, I wasn't mentally ready for the work required, so it was in 2018 that I started with course 1.

It took a few months with the Golden Milk and the other products included in Course 1, and my memory started to get a little better. You shouldn't be in a hurry when you go through school, and you have to expect setbacks. In each course, the body reacts differently to the purges. I have had migraines, fevers, various infections in the stomach and body, flu etc. But I've been happy for all the reactions, as it was the result of the body clearing out toxins that should not have been there in the first place.

I've slowly made my way through the entire school, and by June 2020, I could say I'm fully recovered.

I know the culprit of my Fatigue - mold in the kitchen floor after the pipe which had been leaking for a long time broke. My body was warning me, but I did not know how to listen.

To those of you who don't believe in USM (utmattningsskolan.se) , I would still suggest to give it a try. For me, it was rescue after hopelessness and three rounds of sick leave, which did not help. During the sick leave, I was advised to move, which made me even worse. I hardly remember how I was able to take care of my son, who at the time was very young. Being burned out and a single mom is not a good combination.

Now, I have a lot more energy and have I've also started to speak up at work. Everyone is shocked how I've become after UMS, but now I can stand my ground in the workplace.

Today, I still use some things from the UMS program. I drink lemon water every morning. I make ginger shots for the winters. I eat ginger, garlic, and turmeric every day.

I still have to take it easy and remind myself that I've been sick for years. I don't want to go there again.

Thank you, Lena. You have changeed my life for the better.

Sincerely
Monika

I asked Monica in April 2022 how she is doing now, several years later.

"Now I feel pretty good, compared to before, and I'm working full time again. I was sick from 2007 to 2020. During that period, I was on sick leave for Fatigue and work-related stress three regrets. My disease roots were mold and medicine poisoning. "

Berit Roth wants to give the disease a face

UMS member Berith Roth has spoken out in the local newspaper about her Fatigue, and about UMS.

It's probably the case that we must "deliver" a lot of healthy and recovered members, before the take can be turned, from "it's mental illness" over to "best we investigate because it can be very much; mold, parasites, copper-uranium poisonings, apart viruses".

I asked before this e-book how it is now many years later:

"I'm feeling pretty good, and I've got a 50% job! I feel like that's enough for me! I've been working half-time since 2018!

I only went on sick leave three months ago, and the Swedish Social Insurance Agency chased me a blowtorch!

However, I was very lucky that I had a very helpful person at the employment agency who helped me with a large team but doctors, physiotherapists, occupational therapists and certainly twenty people who had been involved until 2019 when I was granted 50% sickness compensation.

I went into job training all the time until I got hired in 2018. I didn't have to be on sick leave even though I really needed to rest for a couple of years!

The healing took significantly longer! I sold my house in 2018 and ended up in an apartment that had a mold and water damage! I moved out after a year when it was discovered in my kitchen!

I am much better now, have started to cope with strength training, and can do my job well! I'm working now in June as well!

I had a very great benefit from the School of Fatigue! The brain fog disappeared first in course 1! I understood how dangerous mold is, and I learned about toxics and started eating better and cleaner, so my hair and nails started to grow better!

Since I made it to the hospital in India, which UMS is collaborating with, I was detoxified. The homecoming after India was amazing! I could do a lot more, could slowly start singing again which I hadn't been able to do before! I barely had the energy to talk before the trip!"

What about those who have left us?

UMS is not suitable for all, and some people do not complete the course. Many of the people who have left UMS have done so silently, but I did have the opportunity to speak with some of them.

- Hard to replace the 30-40-50 year recognizable headache tablet with water and salt!

- Hard not to buy chemical strawberries...

- I don't believe that...

But, if you want to get to the stage of healing that the members who spoke in this book have achieved, you must learn a lot of new things, replace one product at a time, and cleanse your entire living environment of toxins. The uphill climb feels tough because it takes a while before the reward comes in the form of well-being.

We interpret the rabble quickly from the social-psychic perspective as lazy, stupid, tricky. What has happened to them is probably that their pineal gland is completely out of joint. It is considered one of the most important organs of the human body, and new research shows that it is the only organ in the body that is interconnected with all the cells.

I will sit down in the year 2023-24 and interview lots of Asian doctors to see if I can create a pre-UMS course which cures only the disorder of that gland. Right now, this book is my first attempt at that spirit. We'll see if the stories of the healed can get many over the threshold and eliminate the mis recovery that comes with a broken gland.

It is already known that toxins weaken it, and this also includes alcohol, which explains that a symptom of addiction is that the chemically addicted basically always feel wrong. In the playlist on YouTube there are a couple of videos about the matter.

Therefore, those who have healed are very important to the school, and I am grateful to those who respond in the Facebook groups and have agreed to interview with me. I know that it is difficult to step up and I realize that my name itself evokes memories of their years of illness...

Most people normally have a tremendous resistance to changing habits, and in this case, you easily become your own enemy. Further, many blindly trust the test results we receive.

I'm only dealing with the sick who are willing to change their lifestyle – and who want to change. I don't know how many people don't go into school, and who think.

- But God, you're going to have to listen to English too! Click a wheel on the bottom of the video, and request translation...

That group never gets in touch with me, and if it did, I'd probably answer;

- Be grateful! Be very grateful that I show videos in English, and not in Hindi or Mandarin, because the bot is very often found in Asia.

I had a relative, poisoned with medicine as few, who received all the courses from me, but who was never able to get out of the Western "pill solution" mentality and probably had three bags full of pills every month. My relative died on March 24, age 61.

The bot is out in the world against "Fatigue" and the school has brought it home. Researchers in Sweden have spoken out that there is no cure, no one has been cured, and this is due, among other things, to the fact that the symptoms are treated solitarily. It is also mistakenly believed that it is "psychological", "work-related" or "social".

So, there should be no problem at all, throwing myself into the program. If I stick only to my relative, who knew me, who had received all the courses, and who died, I can say that there were enormous signs that the pineal gland was completely drugged. It controls what we call common sense, intuition, and it makes sure we can't see real dangers anymore.

I was recovered
in the spring of 2016

At the time, I was then possibly the only one, or one of very few, with Swedish citizenship who was cured.

We have an inflammation of the hippocampus in the brain. The part of the brain that is like a kind of bridge, and a symptom is that we forget. No "new" memories are formed, and there are many of us who do not remember the years of illness at all or even vaguely.

The hippocampus receives information from the levels of different hormones and makes decisions. The adrenal gland, which is often talked about, obeys only orders. The hippocampus regulates temperature, blood pressure, sex drive, hormones, blood sugar and more, and many can get elevated values. The Doctors who consult with us over videos describe the inflammation, and most people recognize themselves in the description.

The doctors in Sweden should know that we get breathing problems because our PH value is wrong, and you can't make a diagnosis simply by asking a person to run up a flight of stairs –

we can't do that. Don't ask a suspected sick person to do that because some of us faint and break our arms and legs. We have a member who broke her back when she fell, when doing her prescribed exercise.

My impression is that in Sweden, doctors treat the breathing problems as "asthma", and it does not cure an incorrect PH value. And the non-existent sex drive as well as the reduced tolerance are diagnosed as "psychological" or "social" and so they send people in on the psyche or to a therapist. The blood sugar weigh-ins are given to "diabetes", and the shifts in blood pressure are given medicine for, abdominal fat man wants to be cured via exercise, and so on, and we never get well.

No one has become so in Sweden either, according to the researchers. You can't dabble with the symptoms, but it requires an overall picture and a holistic approach, and it gives the school.

Researchers say: *"Today, there is no consensus on exactly how burnout should be treated, although it is known that team rehabilitation and work-oriented rehabilitation, among other things, can make people better. Methods used include relaxation exercises, cognitive behavioral therapy, sleep school and coaching."*

In other words, they don't know

Many also tell us that they get psychotropic drugs, therapy, are forced to work out, walk with crutches, etc. It doesn't work with hormonal disorders, inflammations in the brain and poisonings. We can state that there is no cure at all in Sweden

"And because you can't cure it, people relapse, and then it gets worse," says the researcher. "That's the worst thing about this — anyone who has once been burned out carries with them a vulnerability and very easily gets bad again. If this happens, there is a risk that they will collapse completely. So, the prognosis is unfortunately quite poor, therefore it is important to proceed cautiously and not be in too much of a hurry back to work. In many cases, a change of workplace is necessary."

Not causes at all, it's symptoms

One wanted me to forge a group discount agreement with so-called functional doctors, who are generally better for those mimic Asian medicine and thinking and have thus left chemical medicine. I therefore investigated their website, and found that they treat symptoms, not causes at all.

If there is black mold, there are videos about it in the YouTube list, the reason the home generally needs to be changed, or an inner wall demolished, and to get rid of black mold and all furniture, clothes, everything must be sanitized. If the cause is uranium in your own well water, you must stop fetching water there. If the cause is copper, the copper spiral must be replaced or copper pipes in the house replaced.

So, they line up symptoms, and they can certainly suppress or alleviate them, but they don't remove the cause and of course one cannot become healthy. However, I have seen through their newsletter that they are 100% clear that "inflammation is the mother of all diseases", as they have proclaimed, among other things.

"Brain fog – causes

Stress: Prolonged stress has negative effects on the brain. There has been research conducted that shows a connection between long-term stress and damage to the part of the brain that is linked to memory – the hippocampus. Therefore, in many cases, brain fog is stress-related.

An imbalanced gut flora: It may seem far-fetched that the explanation for brain fog would be found in the stomach, but the fact is that there is a strong (and scientifically proven) link between gut flora and cognition. In other words, a poor intestinal flora can lead to various forms of cognitive difficulties, of which brain fog is one.

Nutritional deficiencies: Vitamin B12 in particular has a strong connection to the nervous system. We often see that vegetarians and vegans are deficient in B12, but it can occur even in those who are omnivores.

Poor sleep: Sleep is essential for the brain to recover. It is therefore not surprising that sleep disorders are often linked to various mental illnesses. High-quality sleep is absolutely essential for your brain to function at its peak.

Food hypersensitivity: Hypersensitivity to various foods and additives can affect your general health condition and not least your brain function.

Unbalanced hormones: Hormonal changes can likely contribute to brain fog.

Anaemia: Anemia leads to poorer oxygen transport in the body and general fatigue. Anaemia is usually caused by iron deficiency but may also be linked to vitamin B deficiency and chronic inflammation.

Insulin resistance and obesity: There is a strong link between insulin resistance and cognitive impairment. A well-functioning metabolism is necessary for your brain to function optimally, both in the short and long term. There are also studies that show that the inflammation associated with being overweight can negatively affect the brain. "

It's symptoms, not causes, and that's an essential difference. Black mold behind a wall is a cause, as is uranium in one's own well water, or copper that is broken out in old copper pipes.

There have been many texts about mold poisoning, but that's not because I'm overly fond of that topic, but because that poisoning tops the list of the poison's members have found.

Sick for 17 years, now lecturer

It was in 2001 that I first "hit the wall". I crashed completely; my whole existence contracted into a darkness. I had absolutely no reason to believe anything other than that it was stress and purely psychological. It was "obvious" that it was the work, the home, the living conditions, that were disastrous currently. I promise, it wasn't hard to believe that my illness was due solely to stress.

Never in the fifteen years of illness have I felt better than anyone does two weeks after a severe flu. But when you feel so good, you are almost considered healthy, you are going back to work to some extent anyway. I was working for a period in the middle of these years of illness. I struggled with wage subsidies and recurring sick leave. I collapsed several times a year.

But according to the doctors, I was considered as healthy as I could ever be. Then it slowly started to get worse again, even though I had made my life so much better; I had superb stress-free work that I was able to do with ease, an understanding boss who adjusted the tasks as soon as I got worse, good colleagues, great friends, good relationships overall, and safe home relationship with stable, good partner and safety in myself. Despite all the tools I've been given over the years on how to deal with stress, I just got worse and worse.

I had a very bad memory during these fifteen years, sometimes I've completely forgotten things that I've done. My kids and friends sometimes talk about things for which I was present, and I have no idea what they're talking about. There are gaps from my medical years that are completely black.

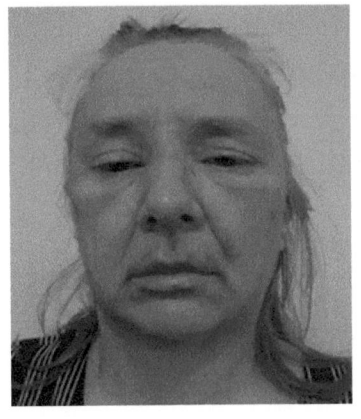

My code for the debit card just disappeared from my brain one day, a code that I had remembered without problems for many years, and I had to order a new card. Once, just before my big crash in 2001, I came at an intersection near where I live and had absolutely no idea where I was going. I didn't know if it was morning or evening, if I was on my way to work, the store, or the day care. I had to look in the back seat to check if I had any child with me.

All the routines that one usually does automatically, such as brushing one's teeth or seasoning the food, were gone. I had a sleep or rest requirement of at least 16 hours a day to function reasonably well, i.e., be able to do anything at all, no matter how small. But I never slept a whole night; I woke up many times and completely lacked deep sleep. I had double beat or irregular heartbeat, constant anxiety, panic disorder. I was bummed, dropping things, hitting, and smashing objects. I had dizziness; it was uncomfortable with climbing stairs because I was scared that I would lose my balance. At some point I also fell and didn't even break my fall with my hands, thankfully not down any stairs.

If I did something too much - that is, anything that would normally be easy to cope with - I got extreme up stress where I could not sleep at all for many nights afterwards. I had a belly that was always screaming. I suffered headaches, eye migraines, and noise and light sensitivity...

It felt like I was in a prison in my own body, and I fantasized about a magic wand that could free me from all my torments, but it seemed to be impossible. I mentioned the flu before, then mix in hangovers, a hearty one, like you've been drinking for a week, even though you haven't drunk at all, and then a few servings of senile dementia and you can maybe understand what I was suffering. Day after day, week after week, month after month and year after year.

When I "celebrated" fourteen years of illness, for the first time in all these years I began to doubt that I would ever be healthy again. I was examined by occupational health care in the spring of 2016. The news was that the doctor had not seen anyone with my medical history recover, ever. I was diagnosed with Fatigue depression, because otherwise the doctor did not think that I would receive sickness benefit, which was considered life. Though I had all the criteria for ME/CFS, what used to be somewhat misleadingly called chronic fatigue syndrome.

I also had severe PTSD, but I was judged to be too ill to cope with treatment for thousands of psychodynamic psychotherapies. The doctor wanted to retire me completely. My ability to work was assessed to be a maximum of 25% because I nagged that I wanted to get back to work. But the doctor warned me and bluntly said that I would be completely bedridden as a vegetable in long-term care if I continued to struggle.

In the summer of 2016, I found utmattningsskolan.se through a group on Facebook. I joined and tried school on the web, even though most of what I thought and knew about fatigue syndrome was turned on its head. At first it felt very strange and different in thinking, but there was nothing that was expensive or even remotely dangerous. I had nothing whatsoever to lose. My prospects, as I said, were not so promising.

Ordinary care also had no help whatsoever to give.

In the School of Fatigue, it is said that fatigue syndrome is due to inflammation in the brain, and it certainly matched my mood - my brain felt like it was cooked in a constant fever. After two weeks, I noticed the first effect of the advice at school. But it took fifteen weeks before my brain was back. Then, I could think, but I was still terribly tired.

I had told myself that it would take time, that there was no quick fix. If I had been ill for fifteen years, I could give two, three years to see if I could possibly feel better. When the brain fog was gone and I could think again, it was time to look for root causes with the help of the school and figure out why and how I had gotten sick.

It took almost two and a half years for me in the School of Fatigue before I could count myself as completely healthy. In January 2019, I was able to completely terminate the cooperation with the Swedish Social Insurance Agency. Now I'm back to full-time employment. The doctor who condemned me looks at me like I'm a walking miracle. But is anyone listening to us?

Some things that I've tried before I've found again in the School of Fatigue. But in the past, it's been like grasping at loose threads without context. It was only through the school of Fatigue that I have found something that has had a whole and a common thread to follow and that has worked overtime.

When I tell some people what I have done to get better, I hear, "Of course it works if you believe it." Well, the placebo effect, the power of thought, is not to be despised as it can heal a lot. Positive thinking is important, without it I probably would not have survived or been able to look for solutions. But just thinking doesn't help. And I've truly believed in all treatment through these fifteen years, from SSRIs to therapy, to vitamins, to meditation and positive thinking. So, if believing when I had SSRIs and therapy had helped me in my illness, then I would have been healthy a long time ago.

Over the years, I have gone to therapy, eaten antidepressants, managed stress, had cognitive behavioral therapy, breathed, relaxed, processed, built self-esteem and self-confidence, changed, and turned around all my life, in and of itself for the better. I have made every attempt to get better. I even changed the diet and made sure to eat well. I phased out SSRIs myself and instead ate B vitamins that worked better. I read about Candida, everything was right, ended up with sugar and fast carbohydrates. Got better from it, for a while. Everything was like that, I got better for a while and then collapsed again.

One of my causes of illness was a stain on the wall at home caused by an old, remediated water leak from the ceiling. It was completely dry, it didn't smell, and seemed like no danger at all. Since moving into the house, I had slowly, slowly gotten worse again in my Fatigue syndrome: increased fatigue, headaches, chronic nasal congestion, often eye migraines. I didn't think about mold.

When we opened the wall, it was all black behind, black mold. Then we sanitized, removed all damaged material, and treated the house with mold-killing agents.

Through analysis, I also found heavy metals uranium in my water. They have only just begun measuring uranium levels in drinking water and only if you ask specifically for them to do it. They say they don't know how it affects people or what dose is harmful.

It was also discovered that I had a gross nutritional deficiency, a stomach that did not absorb nutrition as it should, despite good food.

The Swedish healthcare system does not seem to have sufficient mold experience. For example, when I told my doctor at the health center that I thought the mold that was the cause of me relapsing and getting sicker again, the doctor said "Sure, mold can affect". And in the next breath the doctor asks me "Have you had a traumatic childhood?" In Sweden, it is so inculcated, banked and "determined" that these symptoms are only psychological, so you don't see anything else. Not even when it should be obvious.

When I also told him about my chronic nasal congestion and the mucus in my throat, shouldn't a doctor understand? I know there are the doctors who know this. But I got a prescription for Bricanyl inhaler and cortisone. And so, I would have conversations with a counselor. For my chronic congestion!?

I haven't had a single decline in my well-being since I started UMS and hardly any sick days at all since January 2019, when I first declared myself as healthy.

This is even though there have been fierce battles during my recovery journey, with the Social Insurance Agency and the Swedish Public Employment Service, which could have crushed anyone. Thankfully, I had a boss who fought tooth and nail for my sake. My doctor also tried to support me until he was probably pinched in the ear by the Social Insurance Agency and probably had to try to handle the situation without risking the loss of his medical license.

Fortunately, thanks to UMS, I became healthier and healthier during this period and was able to go back to work step-by-step. What would have happened to me at this point if I hadn't had the school of Fatigue, I dare not think about. But it was still tough and very forced.

They risked spoiling my entire treatment, which I also paid for all by myself. But this is a story that I will tell you more about another time.

My stomach now works, as does my brain, my sleep and recovery, and I've healed and gained more and more energy in the years since 2019. Nowadays, my body tells me I can move. Get out and go get started. When I was sick, there was disaster the times I tried, it resulted in dizziness, that I fell and couldn't even break my fall so ended up with abrasions and broken ribs as a result.

I was thirty-six when I broke through the wall. Before that, since my teenage years, I was exhausted, collapsing at regular intervals and couldn't do anything. My buddies complained to me when I was in my twenties, "You're always tired!"

I found via the analysis we do in course 3 that I had sky-high levels of uranium. Uranium is what I suspect is my original cause of the disease. I grew up in a mountain village, with high levels of uranium in the drinking water. And then lived for many years in my town, where they had to move a brewery because of the high uranium levels in the water. But the population can drink it? And later back to the mining district again...

Mold came in as a disease exacerbator for me only around ten years later.

So, I feel better now than I have in my entire adult life.

I have so much to make up for that sometimes I take in a bit much, lucky that the recovery is now working. I no longer have a hint of "burnout" and I can unwind and sleep well at night even when I've been going a lot. The psychological symptoms such as anxiety, panic disorder and even my PTSD have disappeared. That's without any therapy whatsoever during these years that I've been following UMS.

I now think about root cause, not just symptoms, and how I can fix the problem. When I start to get chest pain, I first think anxiety, stress, and work. Then I think about potassium deficiency since I've had it before. So, I use some potassium salt in my food or eat some supplements. And the pain over the chest disappears regardless of whether the stress changed or not; a pain I had previously had for over fifteen years and thought was psychological. But there it is important to know that you are deficient, because too high potassium gives similar symptoms, and both too high and too low potassium is dangerous to health.

This applies to most of our minerals - it is important to have balance. It is very important to check for physical roots rather that to dismiss the symptoms as psychological during all the years.

The first thing that speaks up if I don't take care of myself is my stomach, and I now listen to it and know what to do to correct it. If there is a cold or stomach flu lurking in the areas, I go into the Fatigue school and read up, and the remedies that are there always work.

The house is fixed in terms of mold, I feel good in it. I have a friend who visited who is mold damaged and she felt significantly better in our house than at her house, so it seems to have worked.

I have recovered from a disease that does not exist with methods that absolutely cannot work. The only people in health care who cared about my results and wanted to know what I've done are the experts who investigated and judged me, the ones who saw up close what was happening. They saw how terribly ill I was and how miraculously healthy I have become.

Unpleasant experience

The prescription of the notorious opioid oxycodone has increased in Sweden. This has led to an increased number of deaths, especially among women and the elderly, a new study[6] shows.

Women get sick faster from poisonings, and according to the doctors I work with, it's because we have a smaller amount of blood. It is faster to poison a woman than a man in general.

Within UMS, we've had a dozen men, but women are absolutely in a clear majority, possibly for the same reason. They fall ill faster and tolerate less.

Those who are called exhausted are a group that almost feels chased by the recipe blocks, and I have been in contact with the National Board of Health and Welfare, which decides, and they

---

[6] https://utmattningsskolan.se/wp-content/uploads/2022/05/Allt-fler-dor-av-okand-medicin-i-Sverige.pdf

possibly listen politely. Still, they should know that inflammation is basically the mother of all diseases.

Someone told me that between 250,000 and 350,000 Swedes can be "exhausted".

I don't think that's enough, and I think of Aftonbladet's claim from 2002, that a million would have been affected then by sick houses, is more accurate.

My seven years of experience tells me that the mold problem is hidden via a sharp cut-off of the international symptom list. Or, as a nurse in a large hospital told me: "Everything we don't know what it is, we shovel to the psyche.

Jag believes that the National Board of Health and Welfare would have to listen significantly better than just politely: Sharp decrease in life expectancy – Sweden stands out.[7]

In the playlist on YouTube there is a video titled: "Brain on Fire Webinar - Brain Changes in Mold Illness with Dr. Mary Ackerley", which details the seriousness:

A co-worker of mine, who was lucky enough to feel like I can mold, wrote: "In February I ended up on the floor, the smallest millimetre I moved cramped my back to the point that I fainted.

---

[7] Sharp decrease in life expectancy – Sweden stands out.

For hours I lay there before the ambulance pumped me so full of various medications that they could not touch me at all, let alone be able to move me to hospital.

Since then, I am impaired in both energy and muscles, constant numbness in the leg and midriff area. "

He was also given the opioid oxycodone but turned it down a little later. I showed the international symptom list to my sick co-worker, who considered that 20 points were correct, and a child has been diagnosed with ADHD, and who is medicated with amphetamines.

A company measured the mold value, over 1.5 is unusual, above 2 is not good and the air is harmful to health above 3.0. In the air, this family had mold levels of 4.2 and in the wall 18.7.

Most UMS members have received psychiatric and social diagnoses, and I was considered to have worked too much. However, all of us have found the root cause and it has never been psychological, social, or work related.

I was warned

There were several people around me who warned me when I mentioned that I was going to create a school of Fatigue on the Internet. They said that "it's just psych cases".

A member of Alcoholics Anonymous, who had 25 years of sobriety behind him, told me that active alcoholics are burned out! He asked to be part of the start, and to see what people wrote, and call in their still drunken "colleagues" who were expected to live with me. There was in the early days none.

We've had three individuals in the first year where both my AA friend and I suspected had substance abuse problems, and we've had someone with a "real" psychosis diagnosis, and for six years in July 2022.

Thus, there are four individuals in six years, 0.66 individuals per year, and enough that they were troublesome, but they by no means overturned the ship.

There are 2,954 individuals who have been in contact with UMS, and of those, four were problematic, and the other 2,950 individuals have had the same attitude as the members who spoke out in the book have.

I don't know how widespread the notion is that "it's just psych cases" is. Even if it's widely spread, I'd say it's a pure myth. There is too much evidence to back it up: we are the norm, rather than the exception.

On the other hand, there are almost no pure active alcoholics, most of them are mixed addicts, and UMS has no medicine cabinets, which is why we are quite uninteresting to that group. On the other hand, it is not a myth that many people have psychiatric diagnoses, and it is probably as one nurse told me: "What we do not know what it is, we shoot to the psyche."

Mold poisonings, for example.

Humanitarian superpower?

I asked one of our veterans, sick for more than ten years but now healthy via the UMS method, and I got the following answer:

"You put a lot of responsibility, and strain on the individual himself. It's psychological, it's in your head, it's your own thinking that makes you sick.

And if that's the case, then you should be to be able to change it and get healthy!? The responsibility lies entirely with the sick person.

Imagine saying that to a cancer sufferer? Or one who lies sick with fever and flu? Or to someone who has a real mental health diagnosis, say schizophrenia.

Clearly, thought and attitude matter, the power of thought is strong. But it doesn't deal with physical illnesses, although it can help manage them better.

Those with the fatigue diagnoses in Sweden are all told that it is their own fault that they are sick.

Many in the surrounding area see it as a pure fantasy, "Pull yourself up!" "How long have you been meaning to be sick?" "

A big explanation for UMS's success story is probably that the sick, who have met my texts automatically, also read about a writer who knows that Fatigue is physically caused, and that symptoms radiate from an inflamed hippocampus, among other things.

The whole UMS is also structured as a kind of self-help group, new questions in the Facebook groups, old ones answered, and if no one answers I do, especially when I am directly addressed:

But you don't get well by hanging out on Facebook... It's in school you must go, utmattningsskolan.se, and after six years I closed our large Facebook group because there were sick people who exclusively stayed there, and you don't get well.

I also met a woman who informed me that she was a UMS member, and I couldn't find her at school! She perceived the group as UMS because she hung out in our largest Facebook group and had done for years. Vi also has debated bans throughout the school, except at the final stage, and given that many have brain fog.

The cleverest thing about the school is that it is a database, an education, which is why it is not even needed more than that. I cure no one, everyone cures themselves, by following the program all the participants in this book have talked about.

UMS Ambassadors

There are three individuals right now who are planning to become UMS Ambassadors in earnest. Two of them are still at the thought stage and Petrea K Marklund has reached action:We are now there that we know that the UMS program holds, and Petrea, who is a teacher at the bottom, has just started lecturing.

Petrea is most easily reached by e-mail:

petrea@utmattningsskolan.se

It's big to get healthy!

Course 1 is available online but is also in the bookstore; "Exhausted & Sleepless: Exhaustion School Part 1: Exhausted – Free of brain fog! Part 2: Sleepless – Free from sleep disorder!" if you experience the online version as difficult.

The online course is the most expensive, as the fee drives the school, but it never becomes an expense because we have many group discounts, which only those who take the online course have access to.

Media and interview requests; kontoret@utmattningsskolan.se and the principal is Petrea K Marklund.

We have many members, who are happy to tell their story!

Lena Holfve

Lena Holfve previously published:

In English:

Exhausted & Sleepless e-book, 2020 Amazon
Exhausted & Sleepless, soft book, (2020) Amazon
Bottoms up, e-book, 2020 Amazon
Bottoms up, soft book, 2020 Amazon

Lena Holfve is a Swedish author who made her debut at one of the largest book publishers, Rabén & Sjögren in 1984.

Lena has several multi translated websites:
www.utmattningsskolan.se
www.utmattad.net
www.sömnlös.com
www.mögelförgiftad.com
www.parasitfri.com
www.cypernboende.com
www.holfve.se
www.lenaholfve.se